Moon-Dog

By **Kate Poels**

Illustrated by
Antonella Fant

Pip went to shut her workshop curtains.

She said goodnight to the Moon, just like
she did every night.

But then, Pip stared in surprise. A star fell
from the sky and landed in her garden.

Moon-Dog

'Moon-Dog'
An original concept by Kate Poels
© Kate Poels 2023

Illustrated by Antonella Fant

Published by MAVERICK ARTS PUBLISHING LTD
Studio 11, City Business Centre, 6 Brighton Road,
Horsham, West Sussex, RH13 5BB
© Maverick Arts Publishing Limited August 2023
+44 (0)1403 256941

A CIP catalogue record for this book is available at the British Library.

ISBN 978-1-84886-982-0

www.maverickbooks.co.uk

This book is rated as: Purple Band (Guided Reading)

She ran outside and saw a dog climbing out of

the star.

"Hello, I'm Pip. Are you okay?"

"Hello," said the dog. "I'm Luna the moon-dog.

I don't know what's wrong with my starship."

"I can help you fix it," said Pip.

"Thank you," said Luna.

Pip fetched her toolbox and went to look at the starship.

"I can see the problem," she said. Pip tweaked with her spanner and tapped with her hammer. "Now try," she said.

Luna started the engine.

"It works!" she said. "You are a star! Now I can go home to the Moon."

"Wow!" said Pip. "I'd love to visit the Moon."

"Would you like to come with me?" Luna asked.

Pip looked up at the big, white Moon.

"Oh, yes please!" she said.

Pip put on Luna's spare spacesuit and they whizzed up into the sky. Pip watched the Earth get smaller as they left it behind.

"We're nearly there," said Luna.

"That's my house."

Luna's garden was very messy.

"Oh no!" she said. "It looks like the cheese noggins have been here."

"What are cheese noggins?" Pip asked.

"They are very naughty creatures," said Luna.

"Look how they've squashed my flowers and broken my swing-seat."

"How do you know it was cheese noggins?" Pip said.

"Look," said Luna. She pointed to a pile of mouldy cheese rinds next to the path. "Only cheese noggins would eat that much cheese and leave their rubbish lying around."

There was a very strong cheesy smell. Pip wrinkled her nose inside her space helmet.

Pip helped Luna tidy up the mess. They put all the cheese rinds into the bin and then Pip mended the swing-seat whilst Luna straightened out the flower beds.

"Thank you," said Luna. "That looks much better. You've been so helpful, Pip. Can I take you out for some moon cake and star juice?"

Pip liked that idea.

"Let's take the moon-scooter," said Luna.

She went into the shed and came back with a

smart-looking scooter.

"It doesn't have any wheels," said Pip with

interest.

"We don't need them," said Luna. "Hold tight!"

Pip stood behind Luna on the scooter and gripped onto her spacesuit. Luna pressed a button and two jets pushed up from underneath. The scooter started hovering just above the dusty, grey road. Luna tweaked a lever and the scooter shot off.

Pip saw colourful creatures as they went past. They all looked very friendly, but Pip couldn't wave. She couldn't let go of Luna.

At last, they pulled up outside the Buzz Café and Luna parked the scooter.

"Hello Buzz," said Luna. "This is my new friend, Pip. Please can we sit in one of the pods so we can take off our space helmets?"

"I'm afraid they're all booked," he said. "It's the cheese festival today and lots of people are coming especially for my cheese tarts."

"Oh," said Luna.

Just then, a big van arrived, and so did a very cheesy pong.

"Thank goodness!" said Buzz. "There's the cheese delivery now."

The driver got out to talk to Buzz, and Luna and Pip went back to collect the moon-scooter.

"We'll have to try another time," said Luna, sadly.

Suddenly, there was a loud shout from the café.
Pip turned around and saw a group of little purple
creatures, giggling and bouncing around the
cheese van.

"It's those pesky cheese noggins!" said Luna.

"Get away from my van!" shouted the delivery man.

The naughty cheese noggins didn't listen though. They jumped into the van and the engine started. Soon, it was speeding off down the road, leaving Buzz and the delivery man shouting after them.

"Quick!" said Luna, pushing the start button on the moon-scooter. Pip held on extra tight as Luna spun the moon-scooter around. They tore after the cheese van.

"STOP!" Luna shouted, but the cheese noggins did not want to stop.

Pip peeked out from around Luna and looked at the cheese van. There was a big battery underneath.

"I think I can stop the van," she said. "But it's going too fast."

"There's a twisty bit of road coming up," said Luna. "They will have to slow right down there."

Pip got herself ready. When the van slowed down, she jumped onto the back and hung on tightly.

The next bend was so tight they had to slow down even more. This was Pip's chance.

She reached down to the battery and pulled hard at the wire until it came free.

The van stopped and the cheese noggins jumped out. They shook their heads at Pip and jabbered at her angrily. But as soon as she took a step towards them, they ran off in the other direction.

"Well done, Pip!" said Luna. "Buzz will be very pleased with us."

Buzz *was* very pleased when he saw Pip and

Luna come back with the van full of cheese.

So was the delivery man.

"You have saved the cheese festival!" Buzz

cheered. "You can sit in the very best pod and

I will bring you the cheesiest tart I can make."

Pip looked at Luna and wrinkled her nose (just

a little) at the thought of all that smelly cheese.

"Thank you, Buzz," said Luna, "but do you

think we could have some moon cake and

star juice instead?"

Moon cake turned out to be the tastiest thing Pip had ever eaten. It was sweet and sticky with little seeds that burst on her tongue, making it tingle.

She took a big sip from her mug of star juice. It was as warm as hot chocolate but tasted even better.

"I like it on the Moon," said Pip, licking the star juice from her top lip.

Luna gave her a big hug.

"You are very welcome to come here whenever you like, Pip. You can be a moon-dog too!"

Quiz

1. What landed in Pip's garden?
a) Cheese
b) A cheese noggin
c) A starship

2. Why was Luna's garden messy?
a) The cheese noggins had been
b) Luna was in a rush to leave
c) There had been a storm

3. What café do Luna and Pip visit?
a) The Noggin Café
b) The Moon Café
c) The Buzz Café

4. Who stole the cheese van?

a) Luna and Pip

b) The cheese noggins

c) Buzz

5. What did Luna and Pip have at the café?

a) Cheese tart and moon juice

b) Moon cake and star juice

c) Lemon tart and hot chocolate

Turn over for answers

Book Bands for Guided Reading

The colour bands on the left side, from top to bottom: Pink, Red, Yellow, Blue, Green, Orange, Turquoise, Purple, Gold, White.

The Institute of Education book banding system is a scale of colours that reflects the various levels of reading difficulty. The bands are assigned by taking into account the content, the language style, the layout and phonics. Word, phrase and sentence level work is also taken into consideration.

Maverick Early Readers are a bright, attractive range of books covering the pink to white bands. All of these books have been book banded for guided reading to the industry standard and edited by a leading educational consultant.

To view the whole Maverick Readers scheme, visit our website at
www.maverickearlyreaders.com

Or scan the QR code above to view our scheme instantly!

Quiz Answers: 1c, 2a, 3c, 4b, 5b